Heroes of the Revolution

Benjamin Franklin

By Susan & John Lee

Illustrated by Richard Wahl

 CHILDRENS PRESS, CHICAGO

Library of Congress Cataloging in Publication Data

Lee, Susan.
  Benjamin Franklin.

  (Heroes of the Revolution)
  SUMMARY: A simple biography of a man whose many
accomplishments in science, writing, social reform,
and politics still influence Americans today.

  1. Franklin, Benjamin, 1706-1790—Juvenile
literature. [1. Franklin, Benjamin, 1706-1790.
2. Statesmen, American] I. Lee, John, joint author.
II. Wahl, Richard, 1939-   illus. III. Title.
E302.6.F8L42 973.3'2'0924 [B] [92]   73-17358
ISBN 0-516-04651-9

3 4 5 6 7 8 9 10 11 12 13 14 15 16 17 18 19 20 21 22 23 24 25 R 75

What do you want to be? Where do you want to live? What kind of job do you want?

All boys and girls dream about these things. Don't you daydream? A daydream means you are thinking about the days and years to come.

Daydreaming is fun. It gives you something to work for. It's good even if you change your dreams many times.

If you want to be a nurse, you must think about what kind of person makes a good nurse. If you want to fly a jet, you must think about what it takes to be a good pilot. Many people become what they dreamed about when they were girls or boys.

This is a story about a boy who dreamed many dreams. It is a true story. It is about Benjamin Franklin, a boy who made most of his dreams come true.

Benjamin Franklin had dreams when he was a man. He dreamed. Then he worked hard to make his dreams come true. This is the story of what happened because of his dreams and his works.

Benjamin Franklin was born in a little house on Milk Street in Boston. It was a cold winter's day in 1706. Your great-great-great-great-great-great-grandfathers and grandmothers were just boys and girls then.

When Benjamin was born, the King of England ruled the country you live in now. There was no United States of America. The people who lived here didn't live in states. They lived in one of the English colonies along the Atlantic Ocean.

The people who lived in the colonies were Englishmen and Englishwomen. Every year people left England to live in the colonies. Ben's father was English. He had left England to start a new life in an English colony.

Benjamin was one of 17 children. His father made candles and soap. He worked at home as most people did in colonial days. Benjamin's mother worked too. She baked bread, made clothes for her children, and helped her husband make a living.

When Ben was a small boy, he worked
very hard to help his father and mother. He
had to bring in wood for the fires. He
helped make the candles and soap. He did
the many jobs people can find for small
boys to do.

Ben had some time for play. He liked playing by the water best of all. Boston was a busy port. Big ships came to its docks. The sailors told stories about their ships and trips. Ben liked to think about the places these men saw on their trips. He dreamed of being the captain of his own ship some day.

Ben was a good swimmer. One day he was flying a kite by a pond of water. Then he went swimming. As he was swimming, he got an idea. He held the string of the kite and lay on his back in the water. The wind blew the kite, and the kite pulled Ben across the water. Ben always liked to try new things.

When Ben was eight years old, his father sent him to school. Ben knew how to read before he went to school. In school he learned to spell and to write. But he did not pass arithmetic. When he was ten, Ben's father took him out of school. It was time to begin work.

Today boys don't go to work when they are ten. They go to school. But in Ben's time, many boys and girls worked. Some children even grew up without learning to read or write.

For two years Ben helped his father make soap and candles. Ben knew he didn't want to make soap all his life. He wanted to go to sea. But his father would not let him. One day, he and his father walked around Boston looking at the work men did in colonial times. They saw bakers, silversmiths, carpenters, barrel makers, and iron workers. But they did not find work Ben liked.

Then Ben and his father went to see his brother James. James had learned to be a printer in England. He now had a printer's shop in Boston. He printed newspapers and songs. Ben had always liked books and reading. So, when Ben was 12, he went to work for James.

J. FRANKLIN
PRINTER

Ben was a good worker. James helped
him learn to be a printer. Ben learned to set
type. He learned how to run a printing
press. He also read many books. He talked
with his friends about the news. He wrote
many stories that James printed in his
newspaper.

As Ben got older, he wanted to be his own boss. James didn't like this. He said he knew what was best for Ben. Finally Ben told James he was leaving. He was going to work for some other printer. James was so mad that he kept Ben from getting a printer's job in Boston. Ben decided it was time to run away.

Ben sold his books to get money. He left Boston and went to New York. There were no printing jobs in New York. Then someone told him there were jobs in Philadelphia.

Young Ben went to Philadelphia. He had
had a hard trip. He was tired and dirty. He
had no clean clothes. He was also hungry.
Ben went to a baker's shop and got three
long rolls. As he walked down the street, a
young girl laughed at the way he looked.
Ben did not care. He was 17 years old and
free of James.

Before long Ben got a printing job. He
worked hard and saved his money. He
went to England and learned more about
printing. On the ship coming back to
Philadelphia, Ben wrote a plan for the way
he wanted to live his life. He liked to put
his dreams into words.

Benjamin had three rules he was to live
by:

— to tell and write the truth
— to believe in what he wrote
— to keep his word when he gave it.

When Ben came back to Philadelphia, he was 26. He went back to work as a printer. Before long, he and a friend started their own printing shop. Ben was now Mr. Benjamin Franklin — and his own boss. Remember the girl who laughed at him the first day he came to Philadelphia? Her name was Deborah Read, but it soon became Mrs. Benjamin Franklin.

As the years went by, Benjamin became a well-known printer. He got lots of work and did it well. One of his jobs was printing paper money. Men asked him to print their books. Benjamin also decided to print a calendar.

Ben called his calendar, "Poor Richard's Almanac." This calendar, or almanac, didn't just list the days, weeks, and months. It also told what the weather might be for each day. Just for fun, Benjamin filled in the empty places on each page with funny sayings.

Many colonists bought Benjamin Franklin's calendar. They liked to laugh at his funny sayings. In one place Benjamin wrote, "A penny saved is a penny earned." In another he told his readers that "Well done is better than well said."

A penny saved is a penny earned

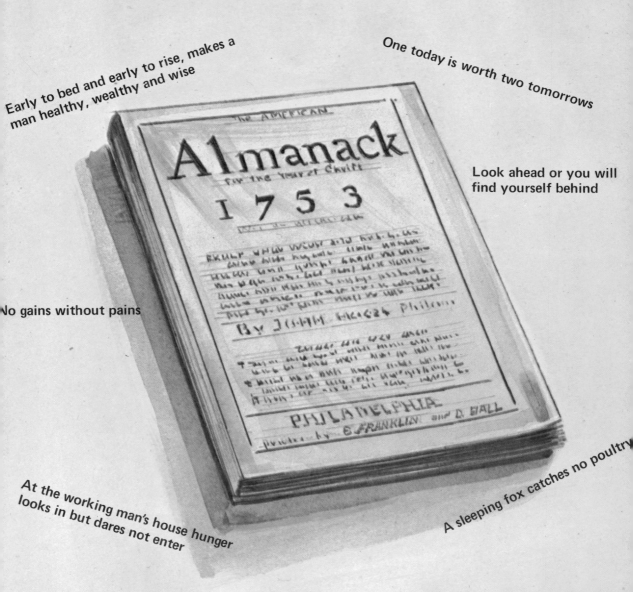

Early to bed and early to rise, makes a man healthy, wealthy and wise

One today is worth two tomorrows

Look ahead or you will find yourself behind

No gains without pains

At the working man's house hunger looks in but dares not enter

A sleeping fox catches no poultry

Well done is better than well said

Benjamin Franklin did many things to make Philadelphia a better place to live. He and some friends started a library. He wanted everyone to read books. He also got the people of Philadelphia to start the first fire department. When a house caught fire, a group of men would leave their jobs and work together to put the fire out.

Benjamin also helped his city by starting a school so boys and girls could learn more things in school than he had. Later Benjamin Franklin helped build the first hospital in Philadelphia. The people were happy with all the things that made their city a good, clean, safe place to live.

Benjamin Franklin did many things for his city, but he still had lots of time. He liked science. He studied in his workroom to find out what made things work. One of the first things he invented was a stove that kept the rooms of colonial houses hotter than other stoves. People called this invention the Franklin stove.

Benjamin Franklin was also interested in the mystery of electricity. In colonial days, many people were afraid of storms and lightning. Some people said that lightning in the sky was a sign of God's anger. They did not know that lightning and electricity were the same thing.

Benjamin was sure that lightning and electricity were the same thing. He was sure that the lightning he saw during a storm was electricity. He wanted to prove that his idea was right. One day, during a bad storm, he and his son William went outside with a silk kite. Benjamin hoped that the kite would draw electricity out of the sky.

They knew this was dangerous. But Benjamin wanted to learn the truth so other people would know what was true. The storm was a bad one. The wind blew hard. In no time at all, the kite was up near the storm clouds. Soon, the string began to burn a little. Electric sparks flew from the key tied to the string. This proved to Benjamin that the lightning he saw in the sky was electricity.

Because Benjamin knew that lightning was electricity, he was able to think up another invention. This invention helped keep people's homes from catching on fire during electrical storms. He put a tall, pointed metal rod on the top of a building. A wire connected this rod with one buried near the house. Then, when there was a storm, the lightning didn't hit the chimney or the house. The lightning hit the metal rod and went harmlessly down the wire and into the rod buried in the ground.

When Benjamin was almost 70 years old, he became known for a new kind of work. In Benjamin's lifetime, more and more colonial people were unhappy with English rule. They did not like King George III. They wanted to be free to run their own country. In 1775, each colony elected some men to meet in Philadelphia. The people of Pennsylvania elected Benjamin Franklin to go to the meeting for them.

The men who met at Philadelphia
decided to break away from England. They
asked Benjamin Franklin and four other
men to write a paper. It would say why the
colonies were not happy with English rule.
Thomas Jefferson wrote the first paper,
and Benjamin changed some of it. On July
4, 1776, the men elected from the colonies
voted to print the Declaration of
Independence.

The English did not like what the colonists were doing. They wanted to keep the colonies a part of England. They would not free the colonies. The American colonists began to fight for their independence.

Benjamin Franklin was too old to be a soldier. But it soon became clear that the colonists needed outside help. They could not beat the English all alone. So Benjamin Franklin was picked to go on a long ocean trip to Europe. He would try to get the French to help the colonists beat the English.

At age 70, Benjamin sailed for Paris, the capital of France. When he got there, everyone wanted to meet him. They had heard about this man who had written funny sayings and who had invented useful things.

The King and Queen of France were dressed in fur, lace, and satin. Other important Frenchmen also were dressed in fine clothes. And what did Benjamin wear? He wore a plain brown suit and his coonskin hat. The people of France liked him. They knew he was a great man even if he did wear funny clothes.

Benjamin Franklin soon talked the French into helping the Americans fight for independence. The French signed a treaty of friendship with America. Not long after, French ships showed up in the harbors of America.

Franklin also got the French king to lend the colonists money for army supplies. The rag-tag American army under General George Washington needed food and clothing and guns. Franklin used his ideas, his funny stories, and his honest ways to get the French to help the Americans.

After years of war, good news came to France from America. The colonists were free! The English army gave up at

Yorktown, Virginia. The French navy
had kept the English navy from helping the
English army. And the French soldiers
helped the American soldiers beat the
English in a fight on the land.

If it hadn't been for Benjamin Franklin,
France might never have helped the 13
American colonies break away from
England. Because of Franklin, the French
helped the Americans win their
independence.

In 1785, Franklin was ready to leave France. He had liked his life there, but he wanted to go back to America. He had been away from home almost nine years. Now he wanted to see the new states in America. He wanted to know how the people felt about being free from England.

On the day he got home, all the bells of Philadelphia rang to welcome him. Benjamin Franklin was a hero. Benjamin thought he could sit down and rest by his fire at last. He was wrong. The people of his new state elected him president (governor) of Pennsylvania.

It took a lot of work to run the state of Pennsylvania. But Benjamin Franklin also found time to help write the Constitution of the United States. It seemed the older he got the more things Benjamin wanted to do. He even found time to talk against slavery in this country. He wanted to stop slavery in all the colonies because he believed it was not right.

Benjamin was 80 years old when he decided to stop working. Even then he kept on doing things. He wrote the story of his life, in which he told about his adventures. In his book, he told his readers what he enjoyed most about his life. He told his readers to lead good lives, to save their money, to work hard, to read books, and to do kind things to help friends in need.

All his life, Benjamin Franklin was both a dreamer and a worker. His dreams came first. Then came hard work.

When he was a boy, Ben dreamed of what he wanted to be. When he was older, and people called him Mr. Franklin, he dreamed of ideas. He worked to turn his ideas into libraries and hospitals and schools. He worked hard and his ideas became new inventions and science experiments.

Lightning rod

Armonica

School ch

Franklin stove

Bifocals

When he was an old man, Benjamin Franklin still dreamed. He dreamed of a free people, of states free of English rule. And after the colonies became free states, he dreamed of the 13 states becoming the United States. He worked for freedom as many men and women worked for freedom. He worked to make the states into the United States.

He was a dreamer who worked to make his dreams come true. Because one of his dreams came true, you are American, not English. A great French writer said Franklin invented the United States. What do you think of that for a boy who dreamed of being a sailor—one of his few dreams that didn't come true?

About the Authors:

Susan Dye Lee has been writing professionally since she graduated from college in 1961. Working with the Social Studies Curriculum Center at Northwestern University, she has created course materials in American studies. Ms. Lee has also co-authored a text on Latin America and Canada, written case studies in legal history for the Law in American Society Project, and developed a teacher's guide for tapes that explore woman's role in America's past. The writer credits her students for many of her ideas. Currently, she is doing research for her history dissertation on the Women's Christian Temperance Union for Northwestern University. In her free moments, Susan Lee enjoys traveling, playing the piano, and welcoming friends to "Highland Cove," the summer cottage she and her husband, John, share.

John R. Lee enjoys a prolific career as a writer, teacher, and outdoorsman. After receiving his doctorate in social studies at Stanford, Dr. Lee came to Northwestern University's School of Education, where he advises student teachers and directs graduates in training. A versatile writer, Dr. Lee has co-authored the Scott-Foresman social studies textbooks for primary-age children. In addition, he has worked on the production of 50 films and over 100 filmstrips. His biographical film on Helen Keller received a 1970 Venice Film Festival award. His college text, *Teaching Social Studies in the Elementary School,* has recently been published. Besides pro-football, John Lee's passion is his Wisconsin cottage, where he likes to shingle leaky roofs, split wood, and go sailing.

About the Artist:

Richard Wahl received his B. A. from Kentucky Wesleyan College, and his B. F. A. from the Art Center College of Design in Los Angeles. Since then he has illustrated many books and magazine articles. Richard is a skilled artist and photographer who advocates realistic interpretations of his subjects. He lives with his wife and two sons in Libertyville, Illinois.